SOCIAL MEDIA

The cause of moral decadence in the society.

JOE WHITE.

Table of content;

CHAPTER ONE

ACQUAINTING YOU WITH THE TERMS.

Social media is a collective term for websites and applications that focus on communication, community-based input, interaction, content-sharing, and collaboration. It is a computer-based technology that facilitates the sharing of ideas, thoughts, and information through virtual networks and communities.
People use social media to stay in touch and interact with friends, family, and various communities.

Moral decadence is described as conduct that demonstrates a love of self-indulgence, pleasure, and money, as well as the process of social customs and values eroding or deteriorating. It is the process of acting in a way that displays a lack of morality. It denotes a severe decline in a society's moral standards. Moral degeneration seems to be a decline in society's moral standards.

Undoubtedly, one of the most fascinating recent developments is social media. It keeps friends and family in touch, provides a practical tool for reflecting on happy memories, and even assists those who are having trouble finding support from others. Social media does have a lot of advantages, but you should be aware that it also has a lot of drawbacks.

Your day can be made more relaxed by the occasional tweet or a few minutes spent looking through your Facebook page. However, it becomes harmful to your mental health when you feel the need to post every ten minutes, check any changes during your lunch break at work, and feel that your life doesn't measure up to those you see on your friends' pages.

If you find it difficult to envision your life without social media, you have undoubtedly been swayed by the enormous influence that these platforms have on people. It's likely that you, too, have encountered some of the drawbacks of social media.

The fact that social media has harmful physical and emotional repercussions may surprise you. Your view of the outside world and of yourself may be adjusted as a result. A lot of us, unfortunately, are all too aware of the negative impacts of social media. Let's examine how social media harms actual individuals daily.

CHAPTER TWO

CYBERBULLYING.

This is an instance of internet harassment or bullying. Cyberbullying produces psychological, emotional, and physical stress, just like other types of bullying do.
Bullying was a practice that could only be carried out in person before the advent of social media.

Online bullying is now a reality, whether perpetrated anonymously or not. Today, everyone is aware of what cyberbullying is, and the majority of us have witnessed some of the negative effects it can have on a person, including increased feelings of sadness and loneliness, a loss of interest in previously enjoyed activities, missed or skipped classes, possibly dropping out of school, poor grades, etc.
While social media makes it simpler to meet new people and establish friends, it also gives vile people a quick and easy way to pick on others. The anonymity that (some) social networks offer allows bullies to earn people's trust before terrorizing them in front of their friends. For instance, they might create a fake profile, appear friendly to a classmate, and then later betray and embarrass them online. Since anyone can create a fake account and do anything without being caught, threats, intimidation, hate speeches, and rumors can be spread to the masses, which creates a situation of unease and chaos in society.

These cyberattacks frequently cause severe emotional trauma and, in some circumstances, even provoke self-harm or suicide in victims. Cyberbullying affects people of all ages, it turns out.

Online abuse may even affect grownups. Because screens obscure our faces, it's easy to behave badly on social media and other websites without recognizing it.

On the internet, people are overly at ease and say things they wouldn't ordinarily say in person. One of the many terrible aspects of social media is that even if you're not the one saying awful things, you're still going to unavoidably be exposed to them.

Whether or not it is intended for you, cyberbullying will make you think more negatively and probably make you feel worse.

CHAPTER THREE

CYBER CRIMES/FRAUD.

The prevalence of the usage of social networking websites in today's digital age has also attracted internet fraudsters to set up multiple social media accounts and join many social media platforms to increase their chance of getting their victims.

According to a cyber security firm Bromium, the same social media platforms that are used to keep up with friends and family have given rise to a huge global cyber-criminal network. According to the Bromium report, nearly 1 out of 5 organizations worldwide are now infected by malware that is shared through social media.
In another academic study by Mike McGuire, senior lecturer in criminology at the University of Surrey,

social media-enabled cybercrime is generating at least $3.25 billion in global revenue annually.

Social media's effect on cybercrime in the current digital era

1. The number of cybercriminals globally has grown due to the widespread use of social networking platforms.

2. Since social media allows for anonymous communication, most online fraudsters can evade detection after taking advantage of gullible victims.

3. Cybercriminals may easily construct a false identity on social media and use it to contact people anywhere around the globe.

4. It is simple to spread malicious software and websites on social media with as many users as possible in a very short period.

5. It is simple for people to spread false information on social media that might endanger national or international security.

6. Because social networking services are so popular, internet scammers may open as many accounts as they want under different names and utilize them for illegal activities.

7. The majority of private, sensitive information is now posted openly on social media. Of course, this makes consumers more vulnerable.

8. The availability of numerous social networking sites makes it simpler for cyber criminals to send fraudulent and unsolicited messages to unwitting victims using their numerous social media accounts.

9. Proliferation of social networking websites has also led to the surge in cyber terrorism.

10. Because the social media platform has developed into a flourishing field for online con artists, the criminal society on the dark web, where cybercriminals acquire and trade stolen sensitive information, is growing.

CHAPTER FOUR

FOMO (FEAR OF MISSING OUT).

This is a phenomenon that gained popularity at the same time as social media started to take off. It comes as no surprise that this is one of the social media's most pervasive negative effects on society.

The term "FOMO" stands for "Fear Of Missing Out," and it refers to the feeling of anxiety you get when you're afraid of missing out on something enjoyable that someone else is doing. You may, for instance, spend the entire day checking your Instagram feed to make sure no one is doing anything fun without you or you might recurrently check your messages to see if anybody has asked you out. You can feel left out if you see images of something enjoyable your friends got to do and you were unable to join them because of a prior commitment.

What you see on social media constantly feeds this dread. You'll have a greater chance of seeing that someone is currently having more fun than you are if you utilize social media more frequently. And that is the root of FOMO.
Social media platforms like Facebook and Instagram tend to worsen FOMO, although the phenomenon

has been for far longer than social media. Your self-esteem may suffer, anxiety may be sparked, and your usage of social media may increase due to the perception that you are missing out on certain things. FOMO can make you pick up your phone repeatedly to check for updates or compulsively respond to every alert, even if doing so puts your safety and that of other people at risk while you're driving, prevents you from getting enough sleep at night, or forces you to put social media interaction ahead of real-world connections.

CHAPTER FIVE

UNREALISTIC EXPECTATIONS.

As most people are probably aware, social media causes us to develop irrational expectations of friendships and life.

A serious lack of online authenticity permeates most social media platforms. People use Snapchat to document their exciting adventures, post on Facebook about how much they love their partners, and flood their Instagram pages with carefully staged images.
However, you have no way of knowing if this whole thing is a joke. Although it seems fantastic on the surface, that person might be deeply in debt, in a tense relationship, or simply desperate for validation through Instagram likes.

One simple way out of this mess is for everyone to quit lying on social media. But in the era of Instagram influencers and YouTubers who earn millions from being inauthentic, that isn't going to happen anytime soon.

Remember an important adage: you should not judge your everyday life against the highlights of someone else's.

CHAPTER SIX

DEPRESSION AND ANXIETY.

Do you browse social media for many hours every day? Spending too much time on social networking sites may hurt your mood. In actuality, those who use social media often are more likely to report having poor mental health, including signs of depression and anxiety. It doesn't take much thinking to figure out why.

Social media lets you see the carefully selected best parts of everyone else's lives, which you then compare to the negatives in your own life (which only you see). Comparing yourself to other people is a sure path to anxiety and unhappiness, and social media has made this much easier to do.

According to recent studies, the more people use social media, the more negative feelings they experience, including depression.

This could be particularly harmful to people who have been previously diagnosed with anxiety and depression.

It has been suggested that these negative feelings and depressive symptoms come from increased social comparisons and a lack of social interaction caused by spending more time on social media. If you're beginning to notice that you're feeling down regularly, recognize that this is one of the negative effects of social media and that it's probably time to take a break.

Also, you're more likely to feel anxious after reading political arguments and doomsday news than you are after seeing fun updates from your favorite musicians or photos of your friends' pets.

CHAPTER SEVEN

GENERAL ADDICTION.

The addictive part of social media is very bad and can disturb personal lives as well, and teenagers are the most affected by the addiction to social media. They get involved very extensively and are eventually cut off from society. It can also waste individual time which could have been utilized by indulging in a productive task or activity.

Because it's so simple to become engrossed in social media activity, people sometimes forget about their actual goals. People frequently aspire for internet popularity rather than setting their sights on the ideal career by developing practical talents.

Setting and achieving objectives requires a lot of effort and drive. When we don't feel like working hard, social media gives us an easy avenue to divert our attention. As a result, we may discover that we just don't complete tasks since finding distractions is so simple.

Social media can be more addictive than cigarettes and alcohol. It has a powerful draw for many people that leads to them checking it all the time without even thinking about it.

If you're not sure whether you're addicted to social networks, try to remember the last time you went a full day without checking any social media accounts. Do you feel rejected if someone unfollows you? And if your favorite social networks completely disappeared tomorrow, would the absence make you feel empty and depressed?

In the end, social media platforms aim to keep you browsing for as long as possible so they can bombard you with advertisements and profit more. These websites demand your attention for as long as possible due to attention economics. You are constantly fed short films by apps like TikTok, which gradually erodes your ability to pay attention.

You don't need to delete all of your social networking accounts just because you've been using social media excessively. It isn't a horrible idea, though, if you believe resigning is the best course of action for you.

CHAPTER EIGHT

NEGATIVE BODY IMAGE.

Speaking of Instagram celebrities, if you look at popular Instagram accounts, you'll find unbelievably beautiful people wearing expensive clothes on their perfectly shaped bodies.

And to nobody's surprise, body image is now an issue for almost everyone. Of course, seeing so many supposedly perfect people (according to society's standards) daily makes you conscious of how different you look from those pictures. And not everyone comes to healthy conclusions in this situation.

The fact that everyone is human must always be kept in mind. Nobody suddenly looks like a supermodel when they wake up on a certain morning, and while many people have worked very hard to build their bodies, not everyone who appears fit has done so. Unhealthy measures have undoubtedly been taken by many people in their quest for social media fame to look more attractive. You won't have to worry about fake Instagram beauty if you surround yourself with people who accept you for who you are.

One's self-esteem suffers as a result. On social media, presenting a particular identity is simple. The nasty stuff in between is often hidden under beautiful holiday images or posts about new babies. We tend to primarily see the positive aspects, which might cause social comparison.

According to one study, "participants using Facebook more often had lower trait self-esteem, and this was mediated by increased exposure to upward social comparisons on social media." This suggests that our self-esteem decreases when we observe the lives of others that we judge to be better than our own.

CHAPTER NINE

REPUTATION DAMAGE AND RELATIONSHIP ISSUES.

Social media can easily ruin someone's reputation; by creating a false story and spreading it across social media. Similarly, businesses can also suffer losses due to a bad reputation being conveyed in the media about the business.

The cry of "fake news" has become commonplace and consumer confidence in even traditional media outlets has been significantly eroded. Unfortunately, false, misleading, or confusing online content can harm your brand's reputation, upset even loyal customers, and can dissuade people from even considering the purchase of your products or services.

Relationship issues;

No good comes out of online displays of jealousy and snooping. It may seem like an easy option when it comes to dealing with relationships, but in reality, it does more damage than good. Studies show that the more a person uses Facebook, the more likely they will be to monitor their partner, which leads to arguments and crumbling relationships. This further leads to a lack of trust and cheating.

Most people, too, have used social media platforms to propose to each other, then go further to marry. However, after some time in marriage, they find out that they were wrong in their decisions, and they divorce.

Through social media, some couples may also start to feel that their partners aren't living up to expectations simply because they have observed their friends' spouses and the extravagant lifestyles they lead. This starts to give them (especially the females) the impression that their situation is bad and that they might have married the wrong person. This will undoubtedly start to affect how they feel about their spouse as they may start to pay less attention to them, put on a fake smile, or give false information.

A couple should avoid this serious issue if they want their relationship to last.

CHAPTER TEN

PORN SITES.

Social media supporters might disagree. Indeed, with the use of social media, it does appear that people have become more social than ever, as people share more photos than ever before. In specific, social media has reduced the need for people to form intimate relationships for sexual purposes. This has arisen mainly due to the large amounts of pornography that are available on the internet and social media platforms.

Research has proven that people are frequently exposed to pornography through web surfing while they are just 13 to 14 years old. According to Arterburn (2013), pornographic viewing ultimately "neuters" the viewer. People are encouraged by pornography to relieve themselves frequently, and when they engage in this behavior, they effectively develop an addiction to it. People look for more specialized hobbies as their pornography addiction worsens.

Pornographic pictures, videos, and links can be uploaded on social media platforms, which greatly influences the lives of teenagers, as they can't concentrate well. The adaptation of people to watching pornography, however, can be quite harmful. This can foster people to have unusual expectations about how women should look and behave. When real women do not act like how women acted in a pornographic video, men tend to become disinterested in real women.

Most people's lives have been impacted by pornography as they start masturbating. Research indicates that masturbation causes 35% of young guys to get prostate cancer. Wow! Such an amount of young guys suffer from this? Consider how important they would have been if they had been free.

Such a condition might result in death and perhaps reduce the labor force of the nation in which they dwell, which would also lower the nation's economic standing and possibly cause the death of additional inhabitants of that nation who perished from hunger or want.

All thanks to social media!

CHAPTER ELEVEN

USING SOCIAL MEDIA IN A BETTER WAY.

We may start by acknowledging the positive outcomes of social media before deciding how to utilize it in a way that makes us feel happy. Positive social movements may thrive on social media, and it can also serve as a hub for people to interact over shared passions and as a resource for isolated areas. There are a few behaviors that might help us use social media more deliberately so that we can concentrate on the positive and avoid the frequent pitfalls:

*Spend less time on social platforms;
One study found that reducing social media use to a maximum of a half hour a day led to a decrease in feelings of anxiety, depression, and loneliness. Phone settings allow our devices to alert us when we've reached our quota for the day — with these benefits top of mind, we can feel good sticking to it.

*Don't scroll first thing in the morning or before bed;

While many of us use wake-up alarms on our devices (making it all too easy to reach for our phones in bed), a constant stream of news, updates, and selfies doesn't typically set the best conditions for winding down or gearing up to start the day. Consider establishing more mindful routines around these 2 daily constants. Screen-free activities like journaling, practicing gratitude, and meditation are great places to start.

Turn off notifications and only check social media at certain times. We all know how easy it is to respond to pings showing us the latest comments or new posts. But in reality, we're the ones in control. Without all that prompting, and with a schedule that you control, you might find that you can avoid a lot of social media anxiety.

*Use social media on a device that's not your phone; When we think about it, do we need access to every social media platform on all of our devices? Try taking a break by removing apps one-by-one from the device you use most (likely your phone) and see if it's easier to find a better balance in your social media use when it isn't always on hand. When we access social media only when we're sitting at a computer, we might find ourselves less concerned with the virtual world, and able to be present with our physical surroundings.

*Create a feel-good follow list;
If the worry is that social media use is contributing to negative feelings, we audit our following list. Unfollow the accounts that might be leading to the negative feelings we've mentioned, and instead follow accounts that make us feel good, provide entertainment, or even help motivate us to reach our goals. We might also try maintaining a profile in which only real-life friends and community leaders are the majority of that new follow list so we can use social media as it was originally intended: to find new friends and maintain bonds when we're apart.

*Be mindful of your social media habits;
Being mindful means being more conscious and aware of our patterns. Since much of our social media use involves mindless scrolling, the best way to take control of our use is to first be conscious of how we're using social networking sites in the first place. To start, ask yourself the following questions:
-What is your pattern of social media use? For example, do you wake up and immediately start

scrolling, do you scroll during breaks, before bed, etc.?

-How much time do you spend daily on social media?

-How do you use social media? Do you use it to see what other people are doing? Or do you use it to communicate and stay connected with others?

-Do you tend to feel better or worse when utilizing social media? Does it lower your self-esteem, cause you to feel depressed, or do you feel better after being on social media?

Once we know our patterns and the emotions involved in our social media use, we can then be more proactive on ways to counteract the negative effects of social media.

*Set limits on the amount of time you spend on social media;
Studies have shown that the amount of time spent daily on social media is associated with negative emotions. A STUDY by Kiera E. Riehms and colleagues published in JAMA Psychiatry found that

adolescents who used social media for more than three hours a day may be at higher risk of mental health problems.
There are several ways to track, monitor, and block the amount of time spent on social media, including several apps. Lately, Instagram also added the "Your Activity" setting which shows the average time you spent on Instagram in the last week. Another way to start setting limits on social media is to implement a few simple rules you can apply to your daily life. For example, two rules that I enforce daily are #1. No scrolling social media within an hour after waking up and #2. Put my smartphone away at least an hour before bed. Other examples include putting your smartphone away when out with others or when eating meals with family. The general idea of this tip is to establish healthy boundaries with our use of social media.

*Know when it's time to stop scrolling;
A lot of our social media use is compulsive. After all, these networks are designed to keep us engaged as long as possible. Therefore, it's important to be aware of the addictive potential of social media sites. We may constantly check social media sites because of the PSYCHOLOGY OF FOMO and

THE POWER OF LIKES. No matter the reason, the moment being on social media starts to trigger negative feelings is the time you need to stop scrolling. For some, that may mean stopping if they're upset that their post isn't getting as many likes as anticipated or noticing that they're constantly comparing themselves to others. For others, it's when they start feeling down because it appears others are doing fun things while they're bored at home. We have the power to exit social media, and the moment we start feeling negative in any way, that's the time to disconnect.

*Use social media to connect with people who inspire you, share similar interests, and provide a sense of belonging;
A way to combat the negative effects of social media is to instead use it in a positive way that strengthens and maintains connections with others. As mentioned in King University Online's PSYCHOLOGY OF SOCIAL MEDIA guide, the mental health advocacy organization Painted Brain has outlined ways that social media can positively impact mental health. Some ideas include providing support groups, strengthening relationships, and socially integrating with similar interest groups. If

we prioritize using social media as a positive space for staying connected, then we will be more likely to filter out accounts, people, groups, and conversations that have the potential to infiltrate the positive networks we've created.

*If an account stirs up negative emotions, then it's time to unfollow;
Because our use of social media becomes habitual, we often forget that we can control what shows up on our feeds. If you find yourself upset after a social media session, consider the networks you use and the people you follow.
If certain people's posts make you feel negative about yourself in any way, then it's okay to hit the "unfollow" button. Social media can influence our mood, anxiety levels, and self-esteem, so taking a few moments to eliminate toxic accounts can be a very simple yet empowering thing we can do for ourselves.

SUMMARY;

Today, social media is a part of our culture and daily lives, so taking steps to be proactive and mindful of how we use it and the way it makes us feel is crucial to avoid the negative effects it can have. Setting limits on the amount of time we spend and taking control of what we see on our feed can ultimately improve our mental health and wellbeing.

If you turn to the same research (and common sense), the recommended amount of time you should spend on social networks is around half an hour per day. As with many other potential ills in life, it's all about moderation.

www.ingramcontent.com/pod-product-compliance
Lightning Source LLC
LaVergne TN
LVHW020537160826
845677LV00015B/4111

9798352318027